Freestyle Champ

# Freestyle Champ

Evan Owen

Illustrated by Dan Pearce

Evans Brothers Limited

Published by Evans Brothers Ltd.
Montague House, Russell Square, London WC1B 5BX

First published 1974
© Evan Owen 1974

Reprinted 1976, 1979

Printed and bound in Great Britain by
Hazell Watson & Viney Ltd, Aylesbury, Bucks
ISBN 0 237 29020 0 (limp)
ISBN 0 237 29043 X (cased)                    PRA 6253

# 1

There I was, thought Christine. Sitting on the edge of the pool in the sunshine. My feet in the water. My eyes closed. Soaking up the sunshine.

Then there were steps behind me. Only Bill, I thought. Only my brother.

He put his hands under my elbows and lifted me up. My eyes were open now.

"Hey! Stop that, Bill!" I shouted. He was grinning all over his face.

Once, twice, he swung me back and forward. Then he let go. SPLASH!

Was I mad! Luckily I had my swimsuit on. But

I could no more swim than fly.

"Hey!" I screamed. "Get me out! Get me out!" I was thrashing about like a dog in a fit. And all Bill did was to stand there laughing.

"Come on!" he said. "Come on, Chris! Get yourself out!"

I did too. Somehow I got to the edge. Then I pulled myself out of the pool.

I was blazing angry. Bill backed away, still laughing. But I went for him, both fists flying.

He held me at arms' length and went on laughing. The tears were rolling down his cheeks. Which made me even more angry.

I still couldn't get near him, though. So I started to cry. With rage.

"I'll never forgive you!" I screamed. "Never, never, never!"

"That's enough, Chris," said Bill, letting me go. "Can't you see what you did just now?"

"Course I can! I got wet. You nearly drowned me. You know you did!"

"Rubbish!" he said. "I was there, wasn't I? I'd have come in if you'd been in real trouble. Well, wouldn't I?"

I had to nod. Of course Bill would have come in for me. But why didn't he?

"No, you little idiot," he said. "What you did, for the first time in your silly life, was SWIM!"

And that is how it all started, thought Chris. I was eight at the time. Bill was twelve.

Now I am nearly sixteen and next month I swim for Beacon Hill Swimming Club. In the area championships.

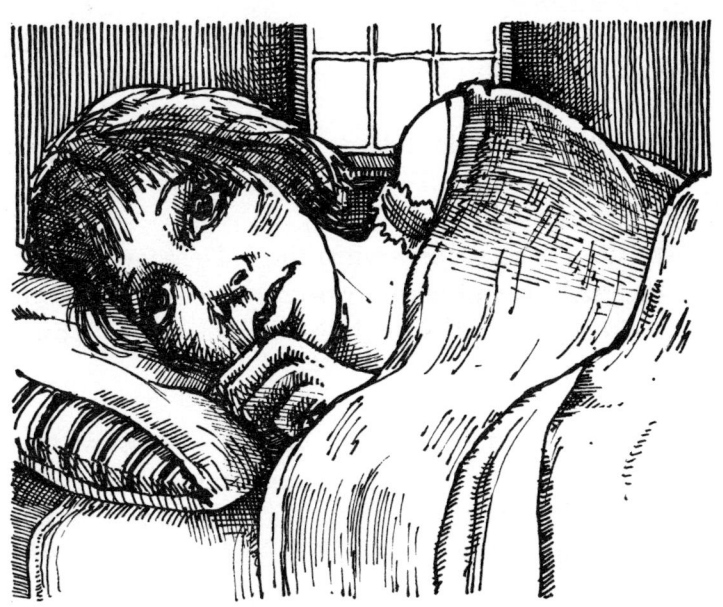

Bill is twenty now. He has been butterfly champion of the area for three seasons.

Christine smiled to herself. It was Sunday morning, she was lying in bed. Thinking about getting up. But there was no hurry.

Mum and Dad always had a lie-in on Sunday mornings. They were not up yet. The house was dead quiet. Chris looked at her watch.

Good. Another half hour at least to lie and do nothing. Except think. And dream, half awake, half asleep.

The watch, too, was something special. She looked at it again.

The glass was scratched, the strap badly worn. Well, she thought, I've had it about seven years.

My first prize for swimming. In a way. Her father had given her the watch when she was able to swim two lengths of the pool without touching the bottom.

Chris opened her eyes wide. The sun was shining through the half-open curtains. She could see a long thin crack in the ceiling. It started at the light fitting in the middle. Looks like a river on a map, she thought.

Like that river I swam in last summer. On holiday. Winding in and out across the fields. Between the trees on one side. And a high bank on the other.

Bill beat me, she thought. He always did. Even in that old river. He's the champ.

It would be great, though, if I could be a champ too!

Me in the 100 metres freestyle. Bill in the 200 metres butterfly. Great!

She sat up in bed and saw herself in the dressing-

table mirror. Her hair all over her face. What a sight!

There's a lot of work to be done yet, she told herself. A lot of hard work.

"I can do it, though," she said, out loud. "If Bill can do it, so can I!"

# 2

Next thing she knew, someone was banging at her door.

"Wakey! Wakey!" shouted a voice. "Breakfast is ready, Chris! Mum says are you getting up this morning? Or staying in bed?"

"Okay, I'm coming. Shan't be long, Rusty," Chris called back. She jumped out of bed.

That Rusty! Always so noisy. But I am late, she thought, looking at her watch. Must have gone to sleep again. Better get a move on.

Rusty was her young brother. He was eleven. His real name was Clive. But everyone called him Rusty. Because of his reddish-brown hair.

Funny thing about Rusty. Swimming did not interest him at all.

Of course, he messed about in the pool in the summer. Making a nuisance of himself. And he could swim enough to get by. But swimming was just not his thing.

He was mad about cameras. Photography. That

was all that really interested him.

Already he had won third prize in a newspaper competition. And what did he do with the prize money? Bought himself a tripod for his camera!

Chris came out of the bathroom, shiny from the shower. Her fair hair flopped around her face.

Rusty should take a picture of me now, she thought. Me in my old dressing gown.

She grinned to herself and ran downstairs, two at a time.

Dad was at the table, behind a Sunday paper. She could hear her mother in the kitchen.

"Morning, Dad," she said. He grinned at her round the paper.

"Morning?" he said. "Nearly afternoon, more like. What time did you get in last night? Or was it this morning?"

"Don't pester her, Joe," said Mrs. Ring, coming out of the kitchen.

"Morning, Mum," said Chris.

"I've made you some fresh tea," said her mother. "You were late, though, weren't you. Bob shouldn't keep you out so late. Where were you, then? All that time."

"Oh, Mum, don't you start!" said Chris.

Mr. Ring laughed. "And you told me to stop pestering her, Alice!" He went back behind his paper.

"It wasn't all that late, Mum," said Chris.

She put some milk on her cornflakes. "And we only went to the disco, as usual. Must have been back just after twelve."

She took a mouthful of cornflakes. Mrs. Ring poured her a cup of tea.

"Anyway, you know I'm all right with Bob," Chris added. "Trouble is, you two go to bed so early. Spend so much time sleeping. We've got better things to do!"

"That's enough of that, Chris," said Mr. Ring, sharply. "What your mother and I do is our business."

"We always have gone to bed early, dear," said Mrs. Ring. "And I'm not getting at you. Nor is your dad. Naturally we worry about you. Wouldn't

be right if we didn't. Now, would it?"

"No, Mum," said Chris, starting on the toast. "Where's Bill?" She could see his place had been cleared.

"Where do you think?" said Rusty. He came in the room with his camera in his hands.

"He's down at the pool. Practising as usual. He would have his breakfast down there if he could!"

"And where do you think you're going, young

man? With that camera?" asked Mrs. Ring.

"Only down to the Town Hall," he said. "There's a rally of vintage cars starting at eleven o'clock. I want to get some pictures of the old crocks. See you!"

"Don't be late, then," his mother called after him. "Lunch at one o'clock, as usual!"

After breakfast, Chris helped her mother wash up. Then she went upstairs to dress.

"I don't like these late nights our Chris is keeping these days," said Mrs. Ring. "Bob ought to know better. Keeping her out to all hours. She's only sixteen. Have a word with him, Joe, next time you see him."

"Oh, all right," said Mr. Ring. "But there's no need to worry. Bob takes good care of her. Jack Mills was only saying the other day: 'Our Bob thinks the world of your Chris.'"

"Yes, I know. I know all about that. But it doesn't alter the fact, does it? Christine is only sixteen. And still at school. She's got her exams to think about."

"All right, all right!" said Mr. Ring, grumpily. "I said I'd have a word with him, didn't I?"

The two families, the Rings and the Mills, had been friends for years. Jack Mills worked with Joe Ring at the car factory at Beacon Hill.

Christine had been friendly with Bob Mills since he left school. He was eighteen now and worked at a TV repair shop in High Street.

He had a sister, Wendy. She was thirteen. A lovely girl with jet black hair. And eyes to match. Rusty was crazy about her.

She knew, of course. He had taken more pictures of her than of anyone. But she thought of him as

just another grubby little schoolboy. Even if he did take a good photo.

If only he was more like his brother, she would think. More like Bill. Then it might be different. But there could not possibly be anyone, not anyone, quite like Bill.

# 3

Later that morning, Christine joined Bill at the pool.

Her brother was practising his butterfly start. This was his weak point. If he could speed up his first few strokes he would knock half a second off his best time.

Greg Scott, the Beacon Hill Swimming Club coach, was at the side of the pool.

"That's enough for now, Bill," he said. "It's getting better, slowly."

Bill climbed out of the pool. He pushed the wet hair out of his eyes.

"Hallo, Chris!" he said. "How am I doing?"

"Not so bad. But you're no world beater. Not yet, anyway!"

"Oh!" said Bill, grinning. "Look who's talking!"

Greg Scott came over to them.

"You're late, Chris! Ten o'clock you said you would be here."

"Ten o'clock, Greg?" said Chris. "Ooh, yes. Sorry, Greg. I forgot and had a lie-in."

"Well, it's up to you," he said, shrugging his shoulders. "If you want to be champ you've got to work for it. And I mean work."

"Yes, I know," said Chris. She was angry with herself. All her great ideas in bed. All about how she would be a champ like Bill.

And the first thing she did was to forget she was due at the pool at ten. A fine start she had made!

Greg could see she was mad with herself. "Not to worry, Chris. So long as you don't make it a habit!"

He laughed. "Why, even the great world champions have their off-days. And I'd bet anything they sometimes forget the time. So you are in good company!"

"But, Greg," she said. "Some top swimmers swim up to eight miles every day. And do nearly a hundred press-ups at a time!"

"Too much for you, eh, Chris?" laughed Bill.

"I should say so!" said Chris. "Ten lengths of the pool and twenty press-ups are about my limit!"

"And mine," said Bill. "But it's harder work with the butterfly. Takes more out of you. So ten of my butterfly lengths are like twenty of your freestyle lengths, Chris!"

"So you say!" laughed Christine. She turned to Greg. "Well, Greg, is he right?"

"Not really. But the butterfly stroke does take more out of a swimmer than freestyle."

"You think the champions' work programmes sound impossible, Chris," he went on. "Don't forget you have only just started. By the end of the year you'll be getting through three times as much training as you are now."

"Oh, dear! Shall I?" said Christine.

"If you want to be a champ and stay a champ, you will," said Greg. "There are no short cuts."

"Poor old Chris!" said Bill, mocking her. "It's a hard life, sweetie. A proper rat race. Or water-rat race!"

Christine ran off to change and Bill dived back into the pool. He swam lazily on his back for a few

strokes. Then he turned over and went into the butterfly.

He was into his third length when Christine arrived. She went straight to the edge of the pool and dived in.

Then she swam back to the side where Greg was ready for her.

"What do you want me to do this morning?" she asked.

"Do four lengths first. But don't push yourself.

Try to get into your rhythm right away," said Greg.

"Wait a bit, though," he added. "Do you know what has happened to Bob Mills? He was supposed to be here at the same time as you."

"No idea. He said he was coming. But he didn't say when," said Christine.

As she pushed away from the side, she called back, laughing, "Perhaps Bob had a lie-in as well as me!"

# 4

There would be no swimming for Bob Mills that morning.

Like Chris said to Greg Scott, he was in bed. But not for a lie-in. And not at home.

On Saturday afternoon he had been to the match with Bill. It was a good game. Their team had won. Bob was feeling on top of the world.

That night he was taking Chris to the disco. And the next day he would be with her at the pool.

His event was the 400 metres freestyle. He was fast but not fast enough. Good but not good enough.

Greg Scott said it was his technique that was wrong. So he was working flat out in training to get it right.

"Bob, I've got a flat tyre," said his father. Tea was nearly over. "It's the near-side front.

"Went to start the car this afternoon. To take your mother shopping. And there it was. Flat as a squashed tomato."

"So I had to walk," said Mrs. Mills. "Good thing it wasn't raining."

"Why didn't you change the wheel, Dad?" asked Bob. "It's easy enough."

"It's not, you know! Not without a wheel brace. I couldn't find it anywhere."

"Tell you what, Dad," said Bob. "I shan't have time to do the job before I call for Christine. But I'll pop round to the shop and borrow the wheel brace from my van. Then I can do the job first thing in the morning. Before I go to the pool.

Wendy can give me a hand!"

*   *   *

So Bob was up early on Sunday morning. While Chris was still lying in bed day-dreaming about him a few streets away.

The car stood outside in the front yard. Bob soon had the nuts loosened on the wheel with the flat tyre.

Then he got the jack out of the boot. He put it in place under the axle and cranked the car off the ground.

When the tyre was clear of the ground he removed the nuts. He dropped them into the hub cap to stop them rolling away.

It did not take long to fit the spare wheel. He put the four nuts back on with his fingers, loosely. Then he began to tighten them a little with the wheel brace.

Suddenly the car started to move. Bob had put on the handbrake before he used the jack to lift the car. But he had not made sure the handbrake was holding.

He was crouching down by the wheel when the car began to move.

He leaped backwards clumsily and trod on the hub cap. His right leg shot out as he fell on his back.

The car slipped off the jack and trapped his leg. Pain shot up into his brain in a red blaze and he fainted.

Wendy heard him scream. She ran to the window.

"Mum! Mum!" she shouted. "Bob's hurt! The car's fallen on him!"

Mrs. Mills threw open the front door. Bob was

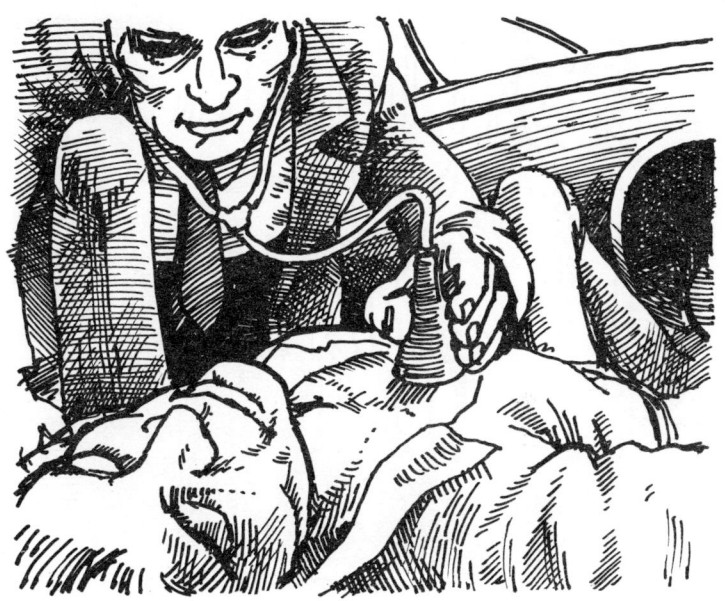

not moving. He was unconscious. A thin trickle of blood was coming from under the car.

She pushed Wendy back into the house. "Go next door. Ask them to ring for help! Hurry!"

A fire engine and an ambulance arrived at the same time. While the firemen lifted the car a doctor bent over Bob.

He was just beginning to come round. "Don't try to move, old son," said the doctor. "We'll soon have you out."

Bob could see his mother behind the doctor. She

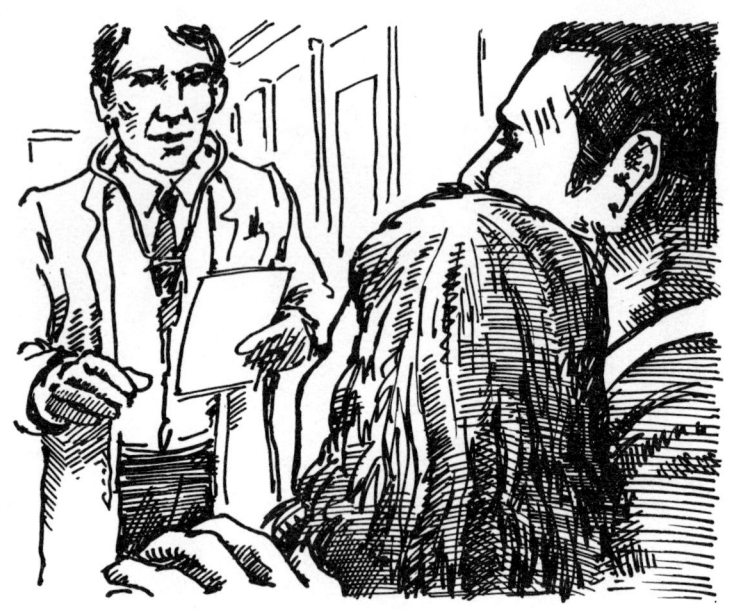

was as white as a sheet. But she smiled at him and nodded. As if to say everything will be all right.

Bob tried to smile back. But a wave of pain flooded over him and he fainted again.

An hour later the doctor came out of the operating theatre at the hospital. He went straight over to Bob's mother and father.

"He'll be all right," said the doctor. "His leg is broken in two places. Badly. But we'll have him on his feet again in a few weeks. So try not to worry."

# 5

It was Rusty who broke the news to Christine and the rest of his family.

He was on his way home from the Town Hall. With his cap on the back of his head, he was walking along, whistling.

He had plenty of time before dinner. So he went out of his way to pass the Mills's house. Hoping to see Wendy. There was always a chance.

This time she saw him before he saw her. And for once she was glad to see him.

She was at the window, white and unhappy. Waiting for her mother and father to get back with news of Bob.

When she saw Rusty swinging along the road she ran to the front door. He grinned happily when he saw her come out and run towards him.

Then he saw her face. She had been crying. "Wendy! What's wrong, Wendy?"

"It's Bob," she said. "He's been hurt. They've

taken him to hospital." She told him what had happened.

Rusty ran the rest of the way home.

Christine and Bill were not back from the pool. He told his mother about the accident. She was in the kitchen getting the dinner ready.

"Oh, dear. I hope he's not too badly hurt," she said. "I'll get your Dad to run me round there this afternoon."

Then the door opened. In came Christine,

followed by Bill. Both of them bright and shiny from their swim.

"Dinner ready, Mum?" she said. "I'm starving!" Then she saw their long faces.

"What's wrong with you two?" she asked. "You burnt the dinner, Mum?" she added, laughing.

"No, Chris. It's bad news, dear. Rusty has just come from Bob's place. He has had an accident."

Chris went white. "Bob? An accident? He's not . . . he's not dead, is he?"

"Hey, steady on, Chris," said Bill. He put an arm round her shoulder. "Tell us what happened, Mum."

When they had heard the story Christine sat down heavily on a kitchen chair. Suddenly her world seemed to have gone mad.

She could say nothing. She could only think of Bob. Lying in hospital. In pain.

It can't be true, she thought. It just can't be true. Not Bob. Not my Bob.

# 6

Mr. and Mrs. Mills had been at the hospital until twelve o'clock. When the Ring family arrived they were still washing up after dinner.

"If you want to go back to the hospital this afternoon, we can take you," said Mr. Ring.

"They asked us not to go again today," said Mr. Mills. "Thanks all the same, Joe."

"Bob is sleeping with all those drugs they've given him," said Mrs. Mills. "They said we can go again tomorrow evening. I wanted to go in the morning. But they said no, wait till the evening."

She sniffed hard and looked ready to cry. "Doesn't seem right somehow. Having to wait till the evening. Why can't I see him in the morning, I'd like to know? Having to wait all that time. It's not right, is it, Alice!"

"It is right, Jean. You know it is," said Jack Mills, gently. "After the operation the boy needs time to recover. He is in good hands. We don't need to worry. He'll be all right."

Chris spoke now, for the first time. "Did they say

he'll be all right? I mean, really all right. Will he be able to swim again?"

"Bless you, dear, of course he will!" said Mrs. Mills. "He'll be right as rain when the leg's mended, won't he, Jack."

Mr. Mills frowned. "Not so fast, Jean, not so fast. He'll be all right, of course, Chris. No doubt about that. But it's going to take time. It's something you can't hurry."

"How long? How long will it be? Before Bob is ready to swim again?" asked Bill.

"They wouldn't say," said Mr. Mills. "The doctor said the bone was badly crushed. They had to put a pin in it, or something."

"He did explain, the doctor," put in Mrs. Mills. "He was very good really. He even drew a picture to show us what he was doing. But we were too upset to take it in properly."

Christine felt a little happier now. Bob would miss the championships but there was always next year. He was going to be all right. That was all that really mattered.

"What about your car, Mr. Mills?" said Bill. "You'll be needing it tomorrow to go to the factory. Dad and me can see to the wheel for you, can't we, Dad? Won't take us long."

"Don't you dare touch that car, Bill Ring!" said his mother. "You must be mad. After what it did to poor Bob!"

"Thanks for offering, Bill," said Mr. Mills. "But a man from the garage up the road is coming to do it for us. Any time now."

"Can I call and see Bob tomorrow night?" asked Christine. "I can call on my way to the pool. Or perhaps I'll skip training for once."

"No need to do that," said Mr. Mills. "They

won't let you stay with Bob more than a few minutes. Anyway, he wouldn't want you to miss training. Well, would he, Chris?"

She shook her head. Of course he wouldn't, she thought. He knows what the championships mean to me. Or what they did mean to me.

# 7

Back home that night, Christine was restless. She could settle down to nothing for long.

There was homework to be done. No escape from that, she thought. Come the end of the world and I shall still have homework to do!

She tried to fix her mind on her work. It was not easy. She kept thinking about Bob, lying there in hospital. But she stuck at it until it was finished.

Then she packed her books in her bag ready for the morning and went downstairs. She went into the living room.

Rusty was watching a play on television with their mother and father. "Where's Bill, Rusty?" she asked.

"Shut up, can't you!" said Rusty. "Can't you see I'm watching this play? Anyway, where do you think he is? It's Sunday night, isn't it?"

"Of course. I forgot," said Christine. "He's round at Jane's as usual."

Jane Young was Bill's girl friend. They seemed

to have been going together for ages. Jane was a member of the swimming club. She was seventeen.

Christine did not think much of Jane. But she was Bill's girl, so she tried to like her.

"Come and sit here, love," Mrs. Ring was saying. She patted the settee next to her. Christine sat down, taking a chocolate from the box her father pushed at her.

She tried to settle down to watch the play. But she just could not get interested in it.

"Think I'll have an early night, Mum," she said, getting up.

"Will you, dear? Make yourself a hot drink, then," said Mrs. Ring. "You look tired, I must say. Haven't got a headache, have you?"

"No, Mum. No headache," said Christine. "I'm just tired." She went into the kitchen and made herself some cocoa. Rusty joined her.

"Hi!" he said. "Made enough for me?"

"I thought you wanted to watch that play," said his sister. "You soon changed your mind."

"Yes. Well, it wasn't much cop. A bit of a drag

really." He stood by the table and played with the sugar bowl.

"I'm really sorry, Chris. About Bob, I mean. I really am."

"Yes, Rusty, I know. Thanks." She smiled at him and gave him a playful punch as she left the room.

It seemed an awfully long time before she could get to sleep.

She lay there watching the lights of passing cars

chasing each other across the ceiling. The muffled sound of the television came up through the floor.

A motor-bike roared down the street. Some boys ran past, laughing and shouting. Somewhere a dog was barking.

Bark, bark, bark, she thought. Why doesn't someone stop it? Take it indoors. Or for a walk. Good thing it's not near the hospital. How could Bob get to sleep with that row going on. Then she fell asleep herself.

Next thing she knew she was in the pool. It

seemed like a race she was in. It felt like a race. But she could see no other swimmers.

I must be leading by a mile, she thought. Must be the last length, too. There's Bob at the finish. Waving me on.

Faster, faster, he seemed to be saying. But she couldn't go any faster. The water was like porridge. Her arms felt too heavy to lift.

She was fighting to keep in front. Fighting to get to Bob before the others. They must be catching up, she thought. But I mustn't look round.

I'm coming, Bob! she seemed to be screaming. I'm coming! But he was getting no nearer.

She was pushing the water behind her like a river steamer. Her lungs felt near to bursting. Why wasn't Bob getting nearer? Why was he getting smaller instead of bigger?

"Bob!" she screamed. "Bob! Bob! Wait for me! Don't go away! I'm coming!"

Christine woke herself up and sat up in bed. I must have shouted out loud, she thought. She felt out of breath and was shivering all over.

Switching on her bedside light she looked at her watch. Ten minutes past eleven. Only just over an

hour since she came to bed.

The television was still booming below. Just as well, she thought. Or they might have heard me.

"This is silly!" she said to herself, out loud. "You won't help Bob this way."

She lay back on her pillow. For a few minutes she let her mind run back over the dream. Then she shivered, turned on her side, and fell into a deep sleep.

# 8

On Monday night Christine arrived breathless at the swimming baths.

"Sorry I'm late, Greg," said Christine. "I called in at the hospital to see Bob."

"Yes, I thought that's where you would be. How is he?"

"Oh, not so bad. They said he's getting along fine. But he'll miss the championships."

"Can't be helped," said Greg. "First thing is to get him fit again. Now you had better get changed. You've a lot of work to do."

In no time at all Christine was at the edge of the pool, ready to dive in. Then Bill came over with Jane Young.

"I thought you would have gone to see Bob to-night," said Christine. "He's supposed to be your best friend." She looked at Jane. "Or had you forgotten?"

Bill went red. "Of course I haven't!" he said angrily. "I didn't go because Mum said you were

going. She said it wouldn't be right for Bob to have too many visitors on his first day."

"Oh, I see," said Christine. "Sorry, Bill! I didn't know. But you will be going tomorrow?"

"Sure," said her brother.

"And I'm going with him," said Jane.

"That will be nice," said Christine. But I don't mean it, she thought, as she dived into the water.

Greg kept her hard at work all the session.

"That enough for tonight, Greg?" she asked. Hanging on to the bar at the end of the pool, she felt too tired to swim another stroke.

"What's that? Enough? Not likely, young Chris! We've only just started."

He crouched on the edge of the pool.

"You're kicking too deep," he said. "That way you're wasting your strength. You'll go just as fast with a shorter kick. And you'll be able to keep it up for longer."

Later, it was her arm movements he wanted to put right.

Oh, dear, thought Christine. Shall I ever get it right? Greg saw her worried look.

"You're doing great, Chris! Don't worry about your arms this evening. Plenty of time to tackle that problem. Just work away at your leg movements. Get those right first."

He grinned at her. "Feeling tired, Chris? Don't you think Shane Gould ever feels tired? Don't you think she sometimes wants to give up?"

"I'm not happy about your breathing, either," he went on. "You're rolling too much with it."

"Perhaps I had better pack it in," said Christine, rubbing the water from her eyes. "Perhaps I'd better take up tennis!"

Greg shrugged his shoulders. "I said it would mean hard work. Well, didn't I ? But it will all be worth it—once you're freestyle champ. And you can be, Chris. You can be!"

# 9

The weeks slipped by. One morning Christine woke up knowing the great day had come.

Today is the day! she thought. The day I have been waiting for and working for. The day of the championships!

Bob's leg was mending well. Now he was walking a little each day with a special sort of crutch.

Christine had visited him every day without fail. Bill, too, had hardly missed a day. He often took Jane with him.

At first, Christine had not liked Jane going to the hospital. But Jane was full of fun. She made Bob laugh a lot. And that is a big help when you are stuck in a hospital bed all day.

So Christine was beginning to think that perhaps Jane was not so bad after all.

Greg was pleased with the way Christine had worked at her training.

"I can't see anyone beating you," he said. "Unless it's that girl from the Tartan Club, Kim

Ferris. She is a slow starter. But she's got the quickest finish I've seen in years."

The area championships were always held at Kenbridge Pool, in the next town. They were the biggest baths in the area.

Christine arrived early with Bill, Jane and Greg Scott. Already the seats around the pool were filling up.

"The place will be packed out before the first race," said Greg. "I've never seen so many people here so early."

"I wonder why," said Jane. "There's nothing special about this year's championships."

There is, you know! thought Christine. At least there will be. If I win. *If* I win? I *must* win!

\* \* \*

Bill's first heat was the fourth race on the programme. He was lucky. The only two men he feared were together in another heat. Dave Walters and Tom Crow.

Bill, too, had been training hard. But not hard

enough to make Greg happy. He thought Bill was getting towards his best form. He did not think he had yet reached it.

"Just do enough to get into the final," he said. "With luck, Walters and Crow will take more out of themselves than you. That boy wonder, Steve Parker, is in their heat, too."

"Steve's not good enough to beat them, is he?" said Bill.

"Probably not. But he is good enough to make them fight for their places. He will make them work hard. And that is what we want!"

Bill won his heat easily. And Greg was right about the opposition. Except for one thing.

Steve Parker came in second to Tom Crow. As only two went into the final, Dave Walters was out.

"Keep your head in the final, Bill," said Greg. "If you do, it's in the bag. Tom Crow took a lot out of himself in that heat. So did young Parker. They should both tire before the last lap."

"Don't let the boy's speed over the first two laps upset you," he added. "Keep well in touch and you should pass him with time in hand."

Before Bill came out for his final, Christine swam her heat. She also won easily. She felt she was swimming better than ever before.

She was feeling very happy. After all, she thought, I've got more than the championship to swim for.

Bob was in the crowd. His mother and father had fetched him from the hospital. He was in the second row, near the finish.

Wendy was sitting in the row behind. And Rusty had grabbed a seat beside her. He had his camera

ready, with plenty of flash bulbs.

Christine could see them all from where she was sitting with the other swimmers. With Bob watching me, she thought, I *must* win.

# 10

There were eight swimmers in the final of the men's 200 metres butterfly.

Bill was drawn on the outside, with Steve Parker three lanes away. Tom Crow was two lanes away from Steve.

"I wish I had been drawn in one of the middle lanes," Bill said to Greg before the race. "It won't be easy, keeping track of the others from the outside."

"That's no problem," said Greg. "You know how to pace yourself. Your finish is better than theirs. Remember that."

The other men were taking off their tracksuits. Bill joined them.

"One other thing, Bill," said Greg. "The water at the edge doesn't get churned up as much as it does in the middle. That should help you!"

A whistle blew. The eight finalists climbed on to their starting blocks.

Suddenly the hum and chatter from the crowd

stopped. There was silence. Complete silence.

This is the worst time, thought Christine, watching Bill from the competitors' seats. This is when you wish you could be anywhere else on earth. This is the time to take deep breaths and concentrate.

Toes gripping the edge of the block. Heels down flat. Leaning forward, ready to dive. Waiting for the starter's pistol. Waiting, waiting, waiting.

It could be anything from two to ten seconds. Eight pairs of heels had to be flat on the blocks.

Only then could the starter get them off.

Steve Parker, tensed up, leans too far forward. He cannot help himself. Into the water he goes.

The other finalists straighten up. And it starts all over again. The waiting.

At last the gun cracks. Eight bodies rocket into the water. Eight swimmers throw themselves into their first strokes.

At the end of the first lap it was hard to see who was in the lead. Bill thought he touched first. So did Steve. So did Tom Crow.

The second length strung them out a little. It was Steve who touched first, with Tom second and Bill third.

There was still nothing in it. Bill was swimming easily. His arms were going strongly through the water, swiftly through the air. He was happy to let the others make the pace.

Two more lengths to go. Young Steve Parker was tiring already. He had fought so hard to beat Dave Walters and make the final.

At the last turn it was Tom Crow in the lead. Steve and Bill touched at the same time, equal second. But Bill was out of his turn before the youngster.

This is it, thought Bill. Now was the time to give it everything. Now was the time all the coaching he'd had from Greg could make the difference. The difference between winning and losing. Between holding on to his championship or just being runner-up.

"Come on, Bill! Now!" shouted Christine. In the stand, Bob was banging his stick on the ground in his excitement.

Mr. and Mrs. Ring were standing up, shouting.

And Rusty was so excited he nearly broke his camera.

Bill was going to win. Halfway down the pool he knew he had the race sewn up.

Steve Parker had dropped right back. And Bill was gaining steadily on Tom Crow.

It was working out just as Greg had said. Tom was beginning to tire badly. He was slapping the water, wasting his strength.

The crowd were cheering them on. The roar of

their voices boomed around the high roof of the pool. Jane was standing up, screaming herself hoarse. "Bill! Bill! Bill!"

He passed Tom with twenty metres to go, to win by a clear second. He was still champ!

Tom swam wearily over to him. "Nice going, Bill," he panted, shaking his hand. "I thought I'd got you beat. But I blew up at the end."

There were two more races before it was time for Christine's final. She left her seat and went back to the changing room.

After the excitement of her brother's win she needed a bit of peace. Away from the heat and fury of the pool she soon calmed down.

In the background the crowd's booming went on and on. But she was thinking about her race. She was trying to remember everything Greg had told her. If only she had listened more carefully!

# 11

The final of the men's 400 metres freestyle was in its last length. The roar of the crowd seemed loud enough to lift the roof.

Four men were fighting for the lead. Then it was all over. The cheering gave way to noisy chatter.

Back from the changing room, Christine looked across to where Bob was sitting. He saw her and waved.

Poor Bob, thought Christine. He should have been in that race.

She looked at the other girls in the race. Any minute now the starter would blow his whistle and she would be on her starting block.

Her stomach seemed full of butterflies. Her heart was pounding away like a tom-tom. She took deep breaths and tried to relax a little.

She wondered whether everyone felt like that before a race.

Christine looked across at Bob. He was leaning

forward, watching her. Then he turned and said something to his mother and father who were sitting behind him.

They looked over towards Christine and waved. Then Rusty saw her and waved. He shouted something but she could not hear him above the din.

Next to Bob, her own mother and father were waving. At least, they will all be cheering for me, she thought. I won't let them down.

Bill came over with Greg. "Good luck, Chris!" said Bill. "Just play it cool and there will be two champs in the Ring family!"

"Well, Chris, you know how to take it," said Greg. "The way you won your heat you've nothing to be afraid of."

"Only Kim Ferris," said Christine.

"Kim? We know she is a strong finisher. But if you get away from her in the first length she'll never catch you."

Then the whistle blew. "Good luck, Champ!" said Greg.

The eight girls mounted their blocks. Christine was in lane four next to Kim Ferris.

For once, it was a perfect start. The eight girls seemed to hit the water together.

Christine was swimming beautifully. Halfway down the first length she was well into the lead.

The roar of the crowd seemed to carry her along. She had only one thought in her head. To get to the turn as fast as she could.

Greg had trained her to use the tumble turn. When she came out of her roll, Kim was only just making her touch. The others were nowhere.

Christine felt full of swimming. She was cutting through the water with a fine rhythm, not wasting a single movement.

Halfway down the pool. Only 25 metres to go! Gulping in air as her head flicked sideways, she saw Kim on her left.

She was catching Christine. Slowly she was inching nearer and nearer.

Bob, halfway out of his seat, bit his lip as he saw Christine's lead being cut down.

All round him the others were shouting: "Come on, Chris! Come on!" But he could only watch, willing her to go faster, faster.

Christine could go no faster. She knew she was forcing herself to the limit.

Kim was up with her now. It seemed to Bob that nothing could stop her going ahead. He wanted to close his eyes, to look away.

Then in the last ten metres Kim lost her rhythm. Suddenly her concentration went. Nobody watching her could see what happened. But she knew. She knew that split second had cost her the championship.

Christine did not know she had won until she

looked up. Greg was leaning over to shake her hand, grinning all over his face. . . . .

"I did it then?" she gasped. Greg nodded happily.

Kim Ferris put a hand on her shoulder. The two girls hugged each other in the water.

"Great swimming, Kim!" said Christine. "I thought you'd got it!"

"So did I," said Kim. "But you were too good for me today. Just you wait till next year! Miss Freestyle Champ!"

\*    \*    \*

Later, when it was all over, Christine was in the back of Mr. Mills's car with Bob. They were on the way back to the hospital.

Christine had never felt so happy. "I still can't believe it's true," she said, holding on tight to Bob's hand.

"It's true enough. I saw it with my own eyes!" laughed Bob. "Though how you held her off I shall never know."

"We've always had this dream, Bill and I," said Christine. She was almost talking to herself now.

"This dream of both being champions. Now it has come true."

She looked up at Bob. "Only one thing spoils it for me. That you aren't champ as well!"

"You just wait!" said Bob. He put his arm round her and pulled her to him.

"The doc says I shall be back home next week. In a couple of months I shall be back in training. Then just watch me! This time next year there will be three champs in the family!"